VELAZQUEZ

PHAIDON

I. Self-Portrait of Velázquez. Detail from Plate 42

VELAZQUEZ

BY XAVIER DE SALAS

WITH FIFTY PLATES IN FULL COLOUR

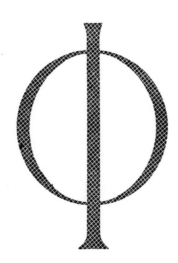

PHAIDON PUBLISHERS INC
DISTRIBUTED BY
NEW YORK GRAPHIC SOCIETY PUBLISHERS LTD
GREENWICH·CONNECTICUT

© 1962 · PHAIDON PRESS LTD · LONDON

MADE IN GREAT BRITAIN

PRINTED BY HUNT BARNARD & CO · LTD · AYLESBURY · BUCKINGHAMSHIRE

VELAZQUEZ

THE REPRODUCTIONS in this volume have been chosen to give an overall view of the art and work of Velazquez. His principal compositions are here; there are several portraits, not only of royalty and high society and of his friends, but also of those deformed and feeble-minded people, the buffoons, who used to live in the palace and were called 'men of pleasure'; there are also some religious pictures and landscapes: we find here examples of every kind of subject which Velazquez painted.

If a similar book had been published fifty years ago, the writer would have extolled Velazquez's naturalism, as did Justi, and Stevenson, and the Spaniards Beruete and Picón. Today we know that this is not enough, and that to understand Velazquez fully, to evaluate him adequately, we must bear in mind other elements of his art. We must take into account his complex intentions, which give a profound double meaning to the things represented.

During the sixty years of his life, with over forty years of artistic activity – for he was precocious in his perfection – he developed his craftsmanship into a supreme skill. At the same time his capacity to see the world and men was continually growing, and with it his capacity to select the images which he translated on to canvas, suppressing everything that was irrelevant to the visual essence of things. But throughout his life Velazquez also continued to enrich his mind with varied reading, and he lived at the court of a powerful monarch and was holding a series of posts in the Palace which brought him closer and closer to the source of power – the King. We must also bear something else in mind while we look at these pictures.

Velazquez was not only a painter, nor did he wish to be considered so. He was charged with important works of renovation in the Alcazar, which required a knowledge of architecture and a strong sense for decoration, and was considered an architect by his contemporaries; recent research has confirmed his activities in this field from 1631 onwards. His library is a proof of how deeply interested he was in architecture.

As a painter he had a studio under him where all work was governed by his personality and manner, which explains many pictures in his style. In addition to his activities as an architect and a painter, he had other tasks at the Palace and was, as his contemporaries testify, a most fortunate courtier, enjoying the confidence of the King, and even his friendship. We must consider the diversity of Velazquez's functions and interests if we want to gain a better understanding of his great pictures than comes from the delight in looking at them. In order to present a complete survey, we must, in addition to the necessary dates, record some details which were unknown to Justi and Beruete and the other critics who wrote at the turn of the last century as contemporaries of the Impressionists.

DIEGO DE SILVA VELAZQUEZ was born in Seville in 1599, a few days before 6th July, the day on which he was baptized at the Church of St. Peter. Velazquez was the elder son of Juan Rodriguez de Silva, an *hidalgo* whose family was of Portuguese origin, settled in Seville since his grandfather's days, and of Geronima Velazquez, his wife, who was of a Sevillian family. The painter took his mother's name from the beginning, which was not uncommon in those days. His parents, though not poor, were not well off. In those days Seville was a great city, wealthy through its commerce with America. From the time of its conquest by the Christians it had been an artistic centre, on the way to becoming the most important in Spain.

At the age of twelve Diego Velazquez was apprenticed to the painter Francisco Pacheco, a Sevillian. Palomino recalls that Velazquez had worked before with Francisco de Herrera the Elder; but it seems that he could not have been with Herrera for a very long time, although he took more from him than from Pacheco.

Pacheco was a mediocre painter, but distinguished and full of erudition. His book on painting bears this out. He also wrote poetry from time to time and his home was a centre of the intellectual life of Seville, visited by the many foreigners passing through. No doubt the young Velazquez attended the academies and discussions held in this literary atmosphere, and their influence remained with him throughout his life.

On finishing his apprenticeship in 1617, he passed his examination as Master Painter, and in the following year, before he was nineteen, he married Juana, the daughter of his teacher. Some verses, recently published, describe the wedding-feast at Pacheco's house and bring out the intellectual disposition of this household. In May 1619 a daughter was born, Francisca; a second daughter, Ignacia, born in January 1621, died very young.

During these early years, while he was still in Seville, Velazquez made a name for himself, fulfilling every hope Pacheco had when he made him his son-in-law. Velazquez's paintings of this period are powerful in design, with dark, predominantly brown colouring giving a heavy appearance, grave and solemn, and very simple in composition. They had a great success.

Very characteristic of these early years are the still-lifes, testifying to a profound study of nature and to great interest in rendering the visual quality of the things represented. That they were successful we know not only from what early biographers record, but also because there are many copies extant. It is interesting that, for reasons to be given later, in most of his early still-lifes, the scheme of his composition is manneristic. As with other painters of this trend, the things which are merely accessory to the theme are in the foreground, and are thus emphasized by their position, while what forms the central theme is relegated to a secondary plane and stands at a distance. The main theme can even be suggested by a picture on the wall. *Martha and Mary* in the National Gallery, London, is the best example of this kind of composition.

We cannot say, however, that Velazquez was a mannerist painter, as we see him from the first straining himself to represent with painstaking naturalism the visible aspects of daily life. Both his temperament and his conception of art divided him from the other Sevillian painters of the time who were following older trends.

Velazquez started painting in brown and greenish dark tones, illuminating and shading the objects in such a way that they stand out strongly from the dark background. This idiom coincided with that of Caravaggio, some of whose works he must have seen, and with that of the Tenebrists, Caravaggio's followers. But Velazquez's work had even then a personal accent.

His still-lifes show the rapid development of his mastery. This can be seen by comparing *Christ in the House of Martha and Mary* (National Gallery, London) with *The Old Cook* (Pl. 2). The same development took place in his early religious painting, leading from the simplicity of the *Immaculate Conception* (Pl. 4) to *The Adoration of the Kings* (Pl. 8) with its more complex composition and its many problems. This shows his precocity, as the latest of these paintings must have been done when he was barely twenty.

From then on Velazquez follows without interruption the way which he has set himself. Volume is rendered in a masterly way, employing less and less the contrast of light and shade, and the rendering of the tones becomes more and more subtle. *The Water-Carrier* (Pl. 6) shows the summit of this evolution. A similar development can be observed in the portraits, as in those of *Don Cristobal Suarez de Ribera* (Sevilla, Chapel of St. Hermengild) and of *Mother Jeronima de la Fuente* (Pl. 9).

In 1622 Velazquez went to Madrid, 'desiring,' Pacheco says, 'to see the Escorial', where so many good paintings were housed, but no doubt also hoping to obtain access to Court. Although he was in touch with some of the Andalusian notables at Court, such as the poet Gongora, whose portrait he painted, he did not do a portrait of the King, Philip III, and returned to Seville. A year later, on a second visit, he was successful. Philip IV had now succeeded his father and had appointed a new 'valido' (the Minister to whom the King entrusted all power), Don Gaspar de Guzman, Count-Duke of Olivares, of an old Andalusian family. Olivares was surrounded by his acquaintances and Sevillian friends, many of whom were linked in friendship with Pacheco. Some of them went to Pacheco's *tertulia* (gatherings), and one of these friends, Don Juan de Fonseca, who held a post at the Royal Palace, was Velazquez's host in Madrid. Velazquez painted his portrait, which was brought to the Palace and much admired by everyone.

This was a turning-point in Velazquez's life. He was appointed to paint the King. There was a sitting on 30th August 1623, and the portrait when finished received the greatest praise. The Count-Duke ordered Velazquez to remain at Court, and from then onwards his life was that of a courtier.

Step by step Velazquez reached an important position in the Palace. He became Royal Painter (6.10.1623), Usher of the Chamber (7.3.1627), and his rights to a daily ration were recognized (18.10.1628). Later he received from the King a *vara de alguacil*, which meant that he could get a yearly emolument from the official who carried out his duties (8.5.1633). Subsequently he became Assistant of the Wardrobe (28.7.1636), Assistant of the Chamber (6.1.1643), Assistant Superintendent of the Palace (9.6.1643), Supervisor of the Works of the Palace (22.1.1647) and finally *Aposentador Mayor* (16.2.1652). But although these posts, which Velazquez held to the end of his life, were posts of responsibility and confidence, they were inferior in importance not only to the two highest in the Court, those of *Camarero Mayor* and of *Mayordomo Mayor*, but also to several others, higher in rank and salary. Velazquez's duties as Aposentador Mayor were simply those of the head of the cleaning services of the Palace, the storing and use of wood and coal, the allocation of seats at the windows on occasion of great festivities, and similar minor functions. In the documents concerned with the grant of this post there is something worthy of note. Not one of the six great officials informing the King about persons suitable for the post of Aposentador Mayor put Velazquez's name first. Some did not even mention him, others placed him third or fourth, and only one put him second; and yet the King appointed him. That proves the King's interest in Velazquez, and the bonds of friendship between them most probably developed during the many visits that we know the King paid in the afternoons to Velazquez's studio to watch him paint.

The same affection is apparent in the constant intervention of the King in the procedure for Velazquez's admission to the Knighthood of the Order of Santiago. As Velazquez could not produce proof of the nobility of some of his ancestors, Papal dispensation had first to be obtained, and then, to overcome a final difficulty, the King granted him the *hidalgia* in order to qualify him for the Knight-

7

hood. At the end of 1659, the Council of the Order of Santiago accepted Don Diego de Silva Velazquez as a Knight. This was not only a title of nobility and a high rank in society, but it also brought its possessor an income.

Philip IV was extremely interested in art and a keen collector of paintings, and he rightly admired Velazquez's art, and this seems the reason why he patronized him in so many ways. About this relationship, and Velazquez's position at the Palace, the Italian Ambassadors are eloquent in the dispatches to their courts about Velazquez's proposed visits to Italy.

As a Royal Painter, Velazquez portrayed his master many times. These portraits have recently been examined by X-rays, and under the final coat of paint of each portrait the King has a very much less regal appearance: softer and sorrowful; the features were painted first in a realistic way and afterwards heightened to emphasize majesty. As the years passed, the King became more and more conscious of the decadence of his dynasty and the decline of Spain, and he felt disillusioned and dissatisfied.

The second portrait of this long series showed the King on horseback, 'everything, even the landscape, imitating nature'. When it was exhibited in 1625 outside the Church of St. Philip, it was admired by everybody and praised by the poets. This large equestrian portrait has disappeared, but we still have other portraits from the following years, not only of the King, but also of the Count-Duke and one of the Infante Don Carlos, standing and dangling a glove with two fingers, a prodigy of elegance without affectation.

The progress reached in these is clearly visible. The silhouettes of the sitters become more and more vibrant and the rendering of volume in space more assured. The subjects stand with restrained gestures, simply in their own atmosphere. No kind of rhetoric has been employed. In a space suggested with extreme virtuosity, the bodies stand out, as the Spanish critic Beruete has said, 'with the most perfect simplicity'. Another new element can be observed in Velazquez's paintings of the late twenties: the general tone is no longer brown; Velazquez is now painting in blacks and greys. He has abandoned the devices of the Tenebrists and starts to follow the example of the great Venetian painters. The royal collection was particularly rich in works of this school. Velazquez was among the many Italian and non-Italian artists then seeking a new path after their Caravaggiesque periods; he is the greatest of all of them and in his work the change of style is most apparent.

In 1627 Velazquez achieved a great success in a competition for a picture to be hung in the Palace, representing the expulsion of the Moriscos (converted Mussulmans) under King Philip III. It was Velazquez's first historical painting. It was lost in the great fire of the Alcazar in 1734 and we possess only a description of it by Palomino. It is described as having in the centre the figure of the Monarch ordering the expulsion, and on the right a matron symbolizing Spain. This device of combining myth and historical facts was a well-established formula, which Velazquez abandoned in his second great historical composition, *The Lances* (Pl. 24), painted a few years later.

The Expulsion of the Moriscos raised him above his fellow court-painters and advanced his position at the Palace, and when Rubens came to Madrid in 1628 on a diplomatic mission, Velazquez was chosen to accompany him on a visit to the Escorial. There is no doubt that the conversation in front of the beautiful pictures of the Royal Collection and of the Escorial must have increased Velazquez's desire to see Italy.

At that time he painted a *Bacchus* (Pl. 10), known today as *The Drinkers* (Los Borrachos), the masterpiece of his first period; soon afterwards he obtained leave of absence and some financial assistance, and embarked at Barcelona with the Marqués de Espinola in August 1629. He stayed some time in Venice and in Rome and visited several other cities. In Venice he saw the large paintings of Titian, Tintoretto and others, whose works at the Alcazar and the Escorial he knew so well. In Rome he remained one year, living at the Vatican and spending the summer of 1630 in the Villa Medici. In one of his early biographies it is said that he copied in Venice one of Tintoretto's pictures, and that in the Vatican he drew copies of the *Stanze* of Raphael and of the *Last Judgement* of Michelangelo. Still in Italy he painted two large canvases – *Joseph's Coat* (now in the Escorial) and the *Forge of Vulcan* (Pl. 12), at the Prado.

On his return he was favourably received by the King, who allotted to him a studio in the North Gallery of the Alcazar. Here the King, as already mentioned, used to visit him. The two pictures that he painted in Italy, as well as the portraits done in the years immediately after his return, show that on his journey he had acquainted himself with the art of his Italian contemporaries, notably Guercino. His palette became richer, his paintings more and more colourful. The contacts with Italian masters in their own country confirmed him in the direction he had already taken in Madrid after studying Titian, Tintoretto and Veronese in the Royal collections. He now modelled not only with shadows but with his colours. The touches of his brush become freer, suggesting but not defining. Commenting on a portrait of this period, Palomino said 'one cannot understand it if standing too close, but from a distance it is a miracle'.

In those years the Count-Duke ordered the erection of a luxurious palace, the Buen Retiro, which was to stand among gardens near the Monastery of the Jeromites and was to be used for important visitors and for great festivities such as theatricals, balls and masques. In 1632 the Count-Duke presented the keys of this palace to the King. In the decoration of the great salon 'of the Kingdoms' Velazquez took part with other painters. He painted a very large canvas immortalizing the *Surrender of Breda* (Pl. 24). This work was finished before 28th April 1635. We see in it the Commander of the Spanish Army, Ambrosio Spinola, receiving the keys of the city from Justin of Nassau. Both Generals are followed by their retinues; in the distant background are the wide plains of the Netherlands and the city of Breda with smoke rising from it.

This time emblematic figures were not employed, and neither the Spanish nor the Dutch are accompanied by classical divinities. A new concept of history painting appears in Velazquez's work and in that of the other artists contributing to the decoration of this salon; only scenes of military life were represented. Some of the pictures in the salon are of high quality, but all of them pale beside that of Velazquez, which is considered by many the prototype of historical painting. There is no rhetoric in it. Both commanders bow chivalrously to each other, offering and receiving the key with restrained and very humane gestures (Pl. 26).

The X-ray photographs of this picture show to what extent its composition was altered during the execution. In the left foreground, forming a first plane, there were originally some seated or reclining figures, whose silhouettes gave depth to the main theme. Seven years before Velazquez had employed the same device in *The Drinkers*, where a figure in the shadow is silhouetted against the shining flesh of the nudes in the lit-up part of the picture. Velazquez overpainted the silhouetted group and, sure of his masterly design, filled the space with the Dutchmen holding their pikes, so balancing the rump of the horse on the right. Thus the eye is carried to the centre, to the principal group, to the gestures equally noble in accepting defeat and accepting victory. The colouring is rich and varied, toned in greens and blues, which is characteristic for Velazquez's work of this period.

The equestrian portraits which Velazquez painted for the Salon de Reinos stand out among the other portraits at the Buen Retiro. In that of Philip III and in those of Queen Margarita and Queen Isabel, Velazquez merely retouched what another painter had done, and gave it life and spirit. The portraits of King Philip IV and of the Prince Baltasar Carlos are by his own hand. *The Prince on Horseback* is a marvel of the painter's art: the face is painted with the greatest freshness, the lively movement of the pony is rendered astonishingly well. The landscape, with the oak trees of the Guadarrama in the near distance, and the blue peaks, partly covered with snow in the far background, broke, up to a point, through the conventions of ideal landscape. Close in time, but drawn with baroque pomp – the most baroque portrait he ever painted – is that of Olivares on a Spanish charger commanding an imaginary army – in fact he had never taken part in any military action. A few years later his long undisputed power was to come to an end. In January 1643, the King dismissed and banished him from Madrid to Loeches, where he died a few months later.

In those years the full-length portrait of Queen Isabel de Bourbon must have been painted, and also that of King Philip IV in brown and silver (Pl. 20), whose richness in tone contrasts with the sobriety of the previous portraits.

Earlier biographers recorded only two visits to Italy: in 1629 and 1649; but a document recently quoted seems to record Velazquez as resident in Rome in 1636, in the parish of San Lorenzo in Lucina. This would explain the replies of some witnesses before a commission of enquiry about his life and family when he applied for admission to the Order of Santiago. Certain other documents also indicate that Velazquez may have had sufficient money for such a journey in 1636: at the end of 1634 he received some substantial payments for paintings, and he also sold his *vara de alguacil* (which, as has been said, had been accorded him in 1633). This stay in Italy could not have been very long: he must have been back in Madrid by the end of 1637, for in January of the next year he was painting the portrait of the Duchesse de la Chevreuse, a beautiful French emigrée.

In 1644 King Philip IV left Madrid for Aragon to help put an end to the war in Catalonia. Lerida fell to the King's army and he entered the city in triumph. At Fraga, a small city not far from Lerida, Velazquez portrayed the monarch in red and silver with the baton of a military commander. This is one of his most beautiful paintings (Pl. 33).

It was perhaps a little earlier that he painted the three royal portraits in hunting dress with guns and dogs of the King, of his brother the Cardinal-Infante, and of Prince Baltasar Carlos (Pls. 22, 23). The colouring is similar to that of the equestrian portraits just mentioned. To these years also belongs one of his finest female portraits, the *Lady with a Fan* (Pl. 35), sometimes believed to represent his daughter. Velazquez painted but few pictures of religious themes, most of them before his arrival at Court. From that time we have the *Christ in the House of Martha*, the *Virgin presenting the Chasuble to Saint Ildefonso*, *The Immaculate Conception* and *St. John on Patmos* (Pls. 4–5), and a series of Apostles, now scattered, of which very few have been traced. After he had settled in Madrid he painted the *Adoration of the Kings* (Pl. 8), and a few years later the most beautiful and serene *Christ on the Cross of San Placido* (Pl. 15). About the time of his first visit to Italy he did *Christ Contemplated by the Christian Soul*, painted in browns and mauve (Pl. 13). A restrained emotion, which has sometimes been interpreted as coolness, pervades all of them.

Later on he painted very few religious pictures, and these have very little connection with each other. *St. Anthony Abbot and St. Paul the Hermit* (Pl. 28) was probably painted in competition, open or tacit, when the Court ordered a series of Anchorites from the best painters in Rome when the

II. Detail from Plate 41

III. Detail from Plate 48

new Palace of the Buen Retiro was completed in 1633. Claude Lorraine, Poussin and Jan Both did large landscapes with small figures of anchorites doing penance or praying in the wilderness. In a similar way, St. Anthony and St. Paul are represented close to a cave, in a wide landscape painted in greens and blues (Pl. 27).

Still later Velazquez did *The Coronation of the Virgin* for the Queen's oratory, with precise skill and elegance, without attempting to avoid conventionality (Pl. 29). Also, whatever may be of the master's hand in *The Temptation of St. Thomas Aquinas* (Pl. 16) must be of this time. Some passages of this painting are of exquisite quality, but others, because of their dryness, raise doubts as to whether they are by his hand. The ensemble is very beautiful, the standing angel exceptional (Pl. 17).

Another of the genres cultivated by Velazquez with originality is mythology. Mention has been made of the *Bacchus* or *The Drinkers*, and of *The Forge of Vulcan*, painted in Italy. To these must be added the *Mars* (Pl. 30), the colouring and handling of which suggest that it was painted before his last Italian visit. On the other hand the *Mercury and Argus*, the only one of the four over-doors painted for the Alcazar which has survived, must date from the very last years of the master's life, to judge by the very loose technique of isolated touches. It has been supposed to be of 1659. In any case, there is no doubt that it represents the final evolution of his brilliant technique, in which he was using so little paint that his touch was a mere rubbing of the canvas (Pl. 36).

To resume the story of Velazquez's life, in 1643 (as already mentioned) he was appointed assistant to the superintendent of the Palace, which meant that he was directing some of the architectural and decorative work done at the Alcazar. His contribution here was important, as he was in charge of the works at the so-called 'Pieza Ochavada', of which he was also appointed *veedor* (inspector). This made him responsible not only for the artistic direction, but also for the accounts and payments, so that he had full freedom to follow his own way.

In order to acquire works of art for the new rooms of the Alcazar, whose decoration was intended to surpass everything in Spain, Velazquez went to Italy again at the beginning of 1649. Provided with letters of introduction and with funds, he embarked at Malaga, and from Genoa he went to Milan, Padua and Venice, where he bought some important pictures. Then he travelled to Bologna, Florence, Modena, Parma and to Rome, where he stayed a long time. There he did one of his most outstanding portraits, that of Pope Innocent X, in deep rich reds, a portrait considered by Sir Joshua Reynolds to be one of the best portraits in the world (Pl. 40). He also painted some papal dignitaries and various members of their families, and the portrait of Juan de Pareja, his slave, pupil and assistant, a picture which brought him the honour of the Academy of San Luca. He also became a member of another body, the Congregazione dei Virtuosi. He was hoping to visit Paris, but the repeated orders of the King, asking for his immediate return, forced him to travel directly back to Madrid in 1651.

In Rome he bought for the King several pieces of antique statuary, some original marbles and some copies cast in bronze. He also brought back moulds of other statues, to be cast in Spain. He bought, too, some porphyry vases and other antiques. The paintings that he acquired for the Alcazar are too numerous to be listed here, but brief reference must be made to those which he painted himself in Italy and brought back to Madrid. Among them are the two small views of the Villa Medici, which bring out better than any other paintings of his the pleasure, mingled with serene melancholy, which Velazquez felt in seeing a landscape. Pictorially they must be considered as advanced as any painted by the Italian, French and Netherlandish painters in Rome at that time. They are not ideal landscapes, but precise renderings of a definite locality; they are landscapes with architecture: one of them represents decaying walls, Palladian arches, topped by a balustrade; the other shows a loggia with a statue of Ariadne in the centre (Pls. 38, 39). Both pictures are studies of daylight, giving the effects of light and shadow, and even the dissolution of colours in the light. That implies that Velazquez was interested in the pictorial problems of landscape painting which were also occupying Poussin and Claude in these years. Velazquez's Views of the Villa Medici are closer to the landscapes of the two French painters than a first glance would disclose. – His beautiful *Venus* (Pl. 37) also owes much to Italy, whether he painted it there or just after his return to Spain. The technique of this picture and the richness of its colouring leave no doubt that it dates from this period of his life. It was not the only nude that Velazquez painted, but the only one that is still extant.

A young woman reclines with her back to us, looking into a mirror held by a little winged Cupid. She is probably a Spanish woman. Her proportions – the small waist, the long legs and her slim 'guitar-like' form – distinguish her from the serene, soft and plump nudes of Venetian paintings, and the undulating lines of her body express tension and restlessness. The tones of the deep reds of the curtains harmonize with the almond-coloured and pink tones of the skin which are emphasized by the dark-greys and whites of the sheets.

It has not been pointed out before that these grey sheets are not just a clever colouristic device, but that they were actually in use. It is recorded that in those years a certain actress in Madrid had 'sheets of black taffeta' on her bed. Ladies of the stage in those days were of easy virtue and used such caprices to show off their beauties.

When Velazquez, back in Madrid, continued his work on some of the most important rooms of the Alcazar, his style of decoration was now inspired by what he had seen in the great Italian palaces.

In the following years he painted some of his most mature portraits. King Philip IV, five years after the death of his first wife, had married Mariana of Austria, his young niece. At Court there was also the young Infanta Maria Teresa, the King's daughter by his first marriage, who was soon to go to France as the wife of Louis XIV, and there were the two young children of the second marriage, the Infanta Margarita and the Infante Philip Prosper. Velazquez painted all these young people, and these portraits are among the most charming and most beautiful of his whole oeuvre. Their baroque pompousness is due to the ladies' fashions of the period, to the large farthingales of the Infantas, to the wigs, laces, ribbons and jewels, but not to the painter. He posed his sitters with great simplicity, using a highly refined technique with the most dexterous touches of the brush and with tenuous paint, suggesting extreme subtlety.

The most important group of these portraits is now in the Museum in Vienna. They were sent as presents to the Imperial Court, which was closely linked with that of Spain. To this group belong two portraits of the Infanta Margarita; judging from the age of the sitter, that with a vase of exquisite flowers must date from 1653 and the other, which shows her dressed in blue, from 1659. Vienna owns also the portrait of the Infante Philip Prosper with his little dog (Pls. 41, 46–48, II, III).

It is difficult to produce a more perfect visual illusion than Velazquez here achieved, or to paint works in which the whole, and each of its single strokes, has such a high pictorial quality. The touches of the brush are of isolated tones with autonomous values, rendering the forms. Distance fuses in the retina these vibrant splashes, which are disposed with the greatest sapience.

Of his final years, coming as the supreme fulfilment of his art, are the two great compositions, *Las Meninas* and *The Tapestry Weavers* (Pls. 42 and 44).

With the *Meninas*, Velazquez achieved at one stroke a masterpiece on a theme always rare in Spanish painting and which, as far as we know, he had not tried before – the family group, in England commonly called 'conversation piece'. The picture shows a simple happening in the daily life of the Royal Family: a visit to the painter's studio of the Infanta Margarita with two of her *meninas* (ladies in the service of the Queen or of the Infantas; from the Portuguese 'meninha', young girl) and with the dwarfs Nicolasito Pertusato and Maria Barbola, and a big dog. This group is bathed in light coming from a side-window. Behind them, in the half-light, are a lady-in-waiting and a *Guarda damas* (gentleman-in-waiting). The child and her retinue are portrayed looking at the King and Queen, her parents, who are posing for the painter; they must be imagined to be standing outside the picture, where we stand when we look at it; the royal pair is reflected in the mirror at the far end of the room. The painter himself, in the second plane, stands before his easel, brush in hand, as if looking at the royal couple – that is at us standing in their place. At the back, a door opens on to a brightly lit staircase and there appears José Nieto, the Queen's *Aposentador*, a silhouette-like figure against the strong light (Pl. 43).

The complexity of this composition must be emphasized: two of the sitters are represented by their reflections only; the group which visually dominates the composition would have had only a subordinate position in real life; and the figure of the painter is given as much importance as any other person in the picture, more in fact than the King and Queen, who appear only in the distant mirror. It is a painting of the act of painting, a moment in the Palace life. It is a painting of an unevenly illuminated room, unequally coloured, with a number of figures, which appear to be casually posed. But in truth the distribution of the volumes is ingeniously planned and the parts closely interlinked, and the visual representation of reality is achieved with the maximum of precision, though the loose technique gives the figures an unprecise contour. They have exact volume, but dissolving into the darkness of the background. The colour, rendered by touches and strokes, seems to have no form or meaning when looked at very close. In this picture exactness has been achieved by evanescence. The whole composition is perfect in design although it appears fortuitous. It appears to follow the rules of court hierarchy; but Velazquez followed the same 'concetto' that he had employed in earlier pictures, relegating the principal theme to the background and giving most prominence in the first plane to what is really secondary.

When life as it was lived at the Alcazar was re-created in this painting, the artist created a world and turned it into art. As the Persian poet Abu Said wrote centuries ago, 'There are moments when I am at the same time mirror, seeing and beauty'. Such a fleeting moment has been made eternal in this painting.

The other great painting of these years, *The Tapestry-Weavers*, represents, as was discovered only a few years ago, a mythological theme, the story of Minerva and Arachne. This fable, pointing the moral that pride will be punished, has been thought by some critics to imply here a political meaning. The incident takes place in the tapestry workshop of Arachne, who was proud of her skill and fame. Once more the same scheme of composition has been employed. The less important figures of the workers form the first plane, and at the back of the picture the tragedy is taking place, in a room, which is smaller and more brightly lit. The goddess is cursing Arachne, watched by three gaily dressed ladies, who are visiting the workshop. These five figures are slightly detached from a tapestry, which forms the background; this light part of the picture contrasts with the half-lit first plane, and the coloured dresses contrast correspondingly with the dark clothes of the workers. If the picture has myth for its subject, it has light for its essence.

In illuminating unequally the two planes of the picture, Velazquez renders space, models the figures and transforms their shapes. Everything has been caught in a fugitive moment. The gestures are wide and transitory. The spinning wheel turns so fast that the spokes disappear. The sun's rays, falling through a window on the left, light up the particles of dust. It is a scene of daily life taking on a mythical significance. Velazquez linked the humble activities of the workers with the aristocratic deportment of the ladies, the simple clothes of the figures taken from ordinary life with the splendid dresses of the ladies and the mythological characters woven into the tapestry which closes the scene (Pl. 45). Reality and fiction combine. The workers, the ladies, the goddess in her armour are presented in the same way. Reality has become poetry, fiction has become real.

It is a work of the painter's last years, and is supposed to have been painted between 1657 and 1660. Before entering into the royal collection it belonged to Don Pedro de Arce, a man of refined taste, who had a good collection of paintings in his home in Madrid, and gathered friends in a literary academy.

In 1656 Velazquez re-arranged the pictures of the Royal Collection which had been sent to the Escorial. In the following year he was planning to go to Italy, but the King withheld his permission, because he wanted to see the decoration of the new rooms at the Alcazar finished. This decoration was being carried out by a team of painters, some from Italy and some from Madrid, who painted mythological scenes on the ceilings of the great salons, under the direction of Velazquez. All of this was destroyed in the great fire of the Alcazar in 1734.

In March 1660 the King left Madrid for Irun, accompanying the Infanta Maria Teresa, and in his retinue was Velazquez. In Fuenterrabia the Infanta joined her bridegroom, the King of France, Velazquez being responsible for all the arrangements of the journey and the ceremonies. On 8th June the King started his return journey and Velazquez was with him, exhausted by his arduous duties. A few days after their return, on the last day of July, Velazquez was taken ill while on duty at the Palace. On 6th August 1660 he died at his home.

Juana, his widow, survived him only by a week. Hers had been a life that passed unnoticed. All we know about her is a few dates and what the inventory of her possessions tells us. She was probably a very retiring woman, to judge by her modest wardrobe, which was certainly much less sumptuous than that of her husband. Of the private life of both, very little is known, and no doubt some significance must be attached to this silence about the great painter.

It happens that we know a lot of tales and gossip about life in Madrid in the time of Velazquez. We possess the letters of the Jesuits, the *Avisos* (Newsletters) written by Pellicer and Barrionuevo, and other texts. The letters alone fill seven large printed volumes, but they contain not a single reference to Velazquez. Rubens visited the Escorial with Velazquez, yet in no letter of the several he wrote from Spain did he mention Velazquez's name. The memoirs of the Marshal Duke of Grammont, who came to Madrid as an Ambassador to settle the marriage of the Infanta Maria Teresa, have not one word about Velazquez, although we know that the painter accompanied the Duke, and received a magnificent present from him. Of Velazquez's visits to Italy we have no reports except some letters about his movements and the letters from the King demanding his return. The person closest to him, who has written about Velazquez, was his father-in-law, Pacheco.

This short biography is panegyrical but gives us no intimate glimpses of his private life. We have also some of Velazquez's own sayings and a number of official documents. In all, the short and scanty references tell us very little about his way of life, his thoughts and his habits.

For Boschini Velazquez was a 'cavalier, che spirava un gran decoro quanto ogn'altra autorevole persona' (a courtly gentleman of such great dignity as distinguishes any person of authority). The King wrote about the painter's 'flema' (phlegmatic temperament). Palomino relates that Velazquez did not like Raphael, although he copied him. There is not much more the sources tell us about him.

We can imagine him grave and ponderous, slow and reflective. A man of few words, perhaps, who lived all his life absorbed in his art and in his court duties. Perhaps he was a homely man – gossip writers record no escapades – most probably a secretive man, who may have been the repository of some of the King's secrets.

From his youth, life brought Velazquez into the confidence of the Monarch, who was a great lover of painting. This confidence made him economically independent through his various appointments in the Palace, allowing him to paint as slowly as he liked and to have a studio in which assistants did the less interesting work; and to the King's confidence, too, he owed it that he was appointed to direct great works of architecture and decoration, and was even given a free hand to apply, as much as he liked, the styles he had seen in Italy.

The inventories made after his death show that he was a man of property. He lived in a large house, better kept than those of more important courtiers, with large and expensive pieces of furniture, silverware, many tapestries and a good library. In 1629, before he left for Italy, the Ambassadors of Florence and of Parma advised their Courts that he should be well received, more because he enjoyed the favour of the King and the Count Duke than on account of his rank at the Court and his fame as a painter. The Ambassador of Florence added that Velazquez should be addressed with 'vos' and that in his presence the Grand-Duke should observe the fullest ceremonial as practised at a royal court, 'for,' he wrote, 'with common Spaniards one's dignity suffers as much by paying them too little respect as by paying them too much respect.'

This despatch was written when Velazquez was only thirty years old. Henceforth the King's favour never diminished, but showed itself more and more. Velazquez was appointed to ever higher posts at Court and about a year before his death was made a Knight of Santiago. His fame as a painter also grew with the years. Even his earliest paintings were much admired and he was able to mature undisturbed and favoured by surroundings which offered him everything he needed.

VARIOUS traits of Velazquez's art have been pointed out in the foregoing pages. It is not easy to define him fully but something more can be added to illuminate the singular character of his art. No doubt, it was of great significance that he spent the years of his apprenticeship in Pacheco's house, where a circle of literary and erudite men gathered regularly. Pacheco's ideas on the art of painting, as known from his treatise, were formed by the mannerist Italian writers, whom he quoted abundantly. Pacheco's art never went beyond them.

But Velazquez did. In his earliest extant works already his aim was to represent plain reality. His still-lifes are naturalistic paintings which show his mastery of tactile values. He probably knew some works by Caravaggio and by some of his immediate followers. In any case, Velazquez employed in several of his pictures what is known as 'tenebrism', though he employed it in his own manner.

All his life his composition followed the schemes of the mannerist painters. He never composed diagonally into the depth, excepting only some of his equestrian portraits.

When he had settled in Madrid and studied the great Venetians, his style changed. His palette passed from brown to greys and blacks. He became more sure of himself, and he succeeded in representing movement. *The Drinkers*, his great composition painted just before his first visit to Italy, reveals another aspect of his development. It is a mythological painting. Iconographically the manner is unique: Velazquez appears to follow the concept of the great Spanish writers who presented the pagan gods as common people living a low life, to show that they were no examples to be followed. Quevedo, Góngora and others wrote in this pejorative sense, and so Velazquez painted the god and his followers as rogues, sitting on a road bank and carousing like vagabonds. To make the painting more humorous, the rogues, who would have been represented humbly by the contemporary *bambocciante* painters in their little pictures, were painted by Velazquez in the heroic manner on a large canvas, life size. He tried to surpass his previous manner, and to paint like the Venetians. The irony in the treatment emphasizes the criticism of the gods. Later on Velazquez went to Italy and came to know her artists, not only those of the past but also those still alive. His palette became richer in colour, a tendency which was to increase throughout his life. His strokes on the canvas became more and more free, and more eloquent in each picture. They were soon to reach a precision that was unique in European painting. Velazquez's bold brush strokes of his mature years can be compared in their eloquence only to those of oriental painters. Like them, he can affirm or suggest whatever he wants by a mere stroke of paint, and all his strokes have a distinctive form and intensity according to the requirements of the things represented.

As the years passed, his art became more complex. He never forgot the use of the *concetti* which he learnt as a youth. In Italy he saw them applied in new ways. There he also found a new respect for mythology: though the gods were criticized, they were generally admitted by the Italians to have symbolic meaning. Thus the nude entered inevitably into his art. We do not know whether Velazquez had tried to paint nudes before he visited Italy, but later he painted several female nudes and more male ones. His travels made him familiar with the intellectual trends of his time, and on his shelves were not only books on art, but some on the sciences and on mathematics, and many more on architecture. His collection of books gives us an idea of the scope of his thought.

His mastery enabled him to render in his paintings not only the figures but also the air surrounding them. The problems of air and light dominate the art of his mature years. In his early paintings he brought out the quality of things, their relation to space, their tactile values; later he represented what was fugitive in them, their momentary and fleeting aspects. His achievement was to paint men and things in their atmosphere, to catch a moment of life that had just passed, and to make it eternal by his genius.

THE PLATES

Peasants at Table. About 1617. Leningrad, Hermitage

4. THE IMMACULATE CONCEPTION. About 1619. Coll. Mrs. Woodall and Miss Frere, on loan to the National Gallery, London

SAINT JOHN THE EVANGELIST ON THE ISLAND OF PATMOS. About 1619. London, National Gallery

6. THE WATER-SELLER OF SEVILLE. About 1619. London, Apsley House, Wellington Museum

7. The Holy Family. Detail from the "Adoration of the Kings", Plate 8

8. The Adoration of the Kings. 1619. Madrid, Prado

9. The Franciscan Nun, Doña Jerónima de la Fuente. 1620. Madrid, Prado

11. THE DRINKERS. Detail from Plate 10

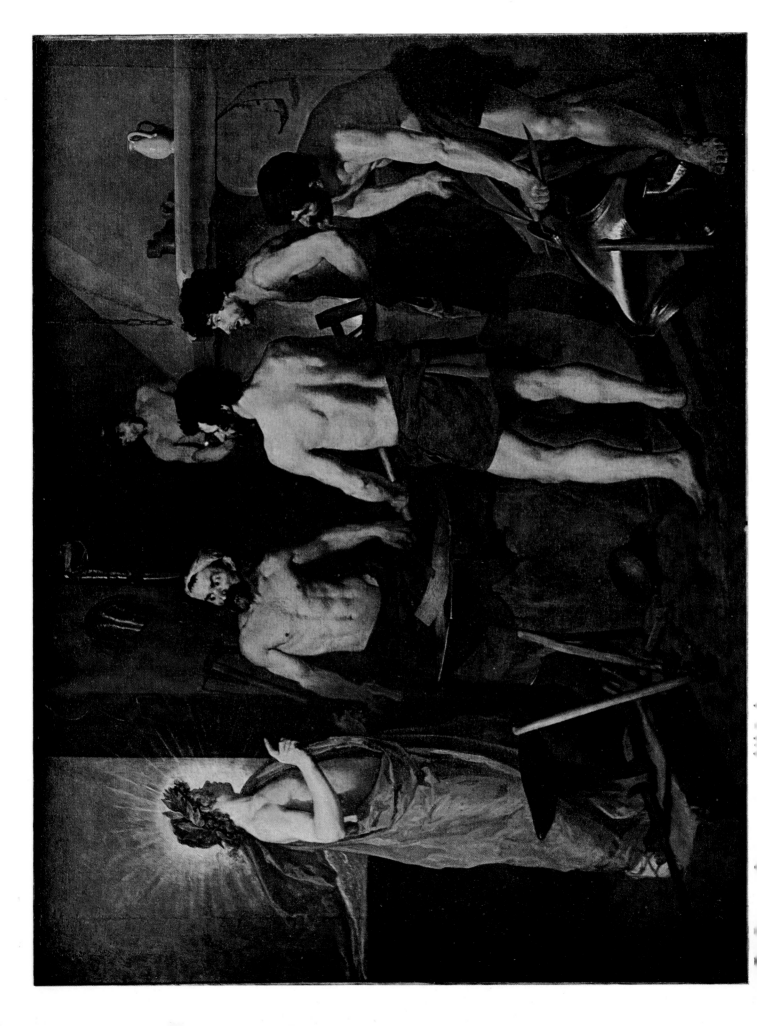

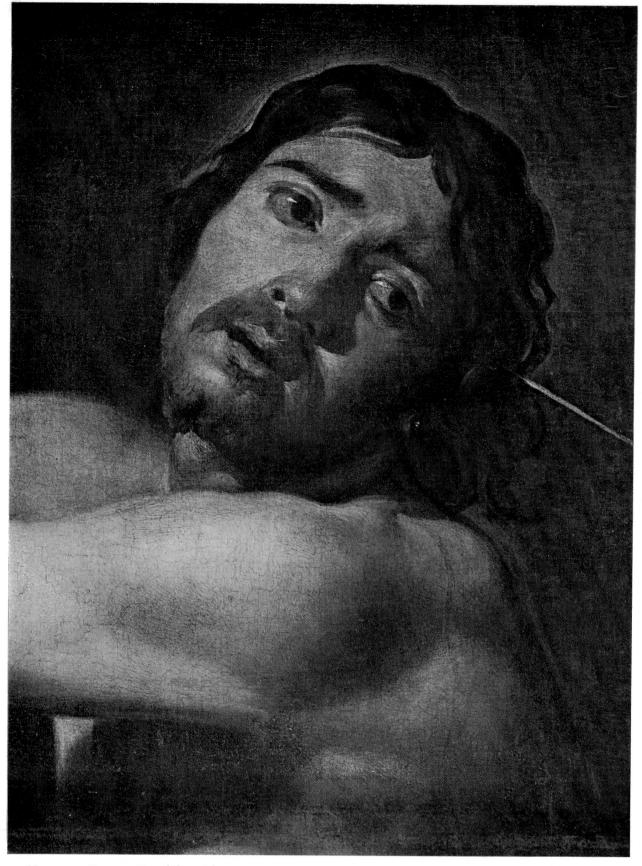

14. Head of Christ. Detail from Plate 13

15. CHRIST. Detail from "Christ on the Cross". About 1631–32. Madrid, Prado

Angel. Detail from Plate 16

18. Prince Baltasar Carlos with his Dwarf. About 1631. Boston, Museum of Fine Arts

. PRINCE BALTASAR CARLOS. About 1632. London, Wallace Collection

20. KING PHILIP IV OF SPAIN IN BROWN AND SILVER. About 1632–34. London, National Gallery

21. THE COURT JESTER DON JUAN DE AUSTRIA. About 1634. Madrid, Prado

22. The Cardinal-Infante Don Fernando as a Hunter. About 1632–35. Madrid, Prado

23. PRINCE BALTASAR CARLOS AS A HUNTER. Detail. 1635–36. Madrid, Prado

24–25. THE SURRENDER OF BREDA ("Las Lanzas"). 1634–35. Madrid, Prado

25

26. Justin of Nassau surrendering the keys of Breda to Ambrosio Spinola. Detail from Plate 24

27. SAINT ANTHONY ABBOT AND SAINT PAUL THE HERMIT. Detail from Plate 28

28. SAINT ANTHONY ABBOT AND SAINT PAUL THE HERMIT. About 1641–43. Madrid, Prado

29. THE CORONATION OF THE VIRGIN. About 1641–43. Madrid, Prado

30. MARS. About 1642–44. Madrid, Prado

33. KING PHILIP IV AT FRAGA. 1644. New York, Frick Collection

34. THE SCULPTOR JUAN MARTÍNEZ MONTAÑÉS. About 1648. Madrid, Prado

36. Mercury and Argus. About 1659. Madrid, Prado

View from the Villa Medici in Rome, Evening. 1650. Madrid, Prado

40. POPE INNOCENT X. 1650. Rome, Palazzo Doria Pamphili

42. THE MAIDS OF HONOUR ("Las Meninas"). 1656. Madrid, Prado

44. THE TAPESTRY WEAVERS ("Las Hilanderas"). About 1657–59. Madrid, Prado

46. THE INFANTA MARGARITA IN BLUE. 1659. Vienna, Kunsthistorisches Museum

7. THE INFANTA MARGARITA. Detail from Plate 46

48. PRINCE PHILIP PROSPER. 1659. Vienna, Kunsthistorisches Museum

NOTES ON THE PLATES

AND

LIST OF COLLECTIONS

ABOVE one hundred original paintings by Velazquez are known today, of which the present selection shows only thirty-six, together with fifteen large details. The reader of this book will look in vain for some of the pictures he might have liked to find reproduced here, particularly the life-size equestrian portraits, which are too large to permit satisfactory reproduction in full colour. (A complete edition of the master's Paintings and Drawings was published by the Phaidon Press in 1943.)

Mr. L. Goldscheider, London, is responsible for the present limited selection of colour plates and for the following short notes.

BIBLIOGRAPHICAL ABBREVIATIONS

KdK = Klassiker der Kunst, vol. VI, 4th edition, Juan Allende Salazar, *Velazquez*, Berlin 1925.

A. L. Mayer = A. L. Mayer, *Velazquez, A Catalogue Raisonné of the Pictures and Drawings*, London 1936.

Lafuente Ferrari = Enrique Lafuente Ferrari, *Velazquez*, Complete edition, with introduction and catalogue, London (Phaidon Press), 1943.

Exhibition Madrid 1960 = *Velázquez y lo Velazqueño, Catálogo de la Exposición* . . ., segunda edición, Madrid 1960.

Palomino = Antonio Palomino de Castro y Velasco, *El Museo pictórico y escala optica*, Madrid 1724.

NOTES ON THE PLATES

. PEASANTS AT TABLE. About 1617. (183×
16 cm.; 72× 45⅝ in.) Leningrad, Hermitage (No. 389).
Until 1895 in the magazine of the museum, where
Wilhelm Bode saw it and recognized it as a work of
Velazquez. (A variant of this composition, but rather
poorly painted, is in the Budapest Museum.)

. AN OLD WOMAN FRYING EGGS. 1618.
99× 116.8 cm.; 39× 46 in.) Edinburgh, National Gallery
of Scotland (No. 2180).
First mentioned by Palomino, 1724. Until 1955 in the
Cook Collection, Richmond. The finest of the *bodegones*
(kitchen or tavern pictures: still-lifes with figures).
When the painting was cleaned in 1957 the date '1618'
appeared.

. MUSICAL TRIO. About 1619. (87× 110 cm.; 34¼
× 43¼ in.) Berlin, Museum (No. 413 F).
Acquired in 1906 from the collection of Langton Douglas,
London. Three old workshop replicas are known; it was
apparently a very popular picture. This composition is
in the spirit, the manner and the colouring of Caravaggio.
Palomino relates: 'Velazquez competed with Caravaggio
in the vitality of brushwork and with Pacheco in
imagination . . . He was called "the second Caravaggio"
because he copied life to perfection and accurately, always
painting every detail from nature.'

4. THE IMMACULATE CONCEPTION. About
1619. (135× 102 cm.; 53¼× 40¼ in.) Collection Mrs.
Woodall and Miss Frere, on loan to the National Gallery,
London.
Pendant to No. 5. – Céan Bermudez (1800) gave a description of both pictures, which in his time were in the
Monastery of the White Friars at Seville. In 1819 the two
pictures were bought by Hookham Frere and taken to
England.
In 1618 Velazquez married Juana, the daughter of his
teacher Pacheco, and it has been suggested that she might
have served as model for the Madonna. The same model,
slightly older, can be seen in plate 7.

5. SAINT JOHN THE EVANGELIST ON THE
ISLAND OF PATMOS. About 1619. (135× 102
cm.; 53¼× 40¼ in.) London, National Gallery (No.6264;
acquired in 1956).
Pendant to No. 4. – Possibly a self-portrait of Velazquez
at the age of about nineteen or twenty, as Allende-Salazar
has suggested.

6. THE WATER-SELLER OF SEVILLE. About
1619. (105× 80 cm.; 41⅜× 31½ in.) London, Apsley
House, Wellington Museum (No.1600).
Listed in the inventories of the Buen Retiro Palace, 1700,
and of the Royal Palace, Madrid 1780.
Joseph Bonaparte, Napoleon's brother, defeated by the
Duke of Wellington in the battle of Vitoria (1813) and
fleeing from Spain in a large travelling-carriage, was
pursued by a squadron of English Hussars. He escaped but
his carriage and other baggage were captured and 165
paintings and other works of art were found, which
Joseph Bonaparte had carried away from the Spanish
Royal Collection. All the pictures painted on canvas were
not only cut out of their frames but even severed from
their stretchers, and were considerably damaged. Among
the 165 pictures were three by Velazquez: *The Water-
seller*, another *bodegone*, and a portrait. The Duke of
Wellington offered to return the art treasures to the
Royal Collection in Madrid, but the King wished the
Duke to keep them.

7-8. THE ADORATION OF THE KINGS. 1619.
(204× 125 cm.; 80¼× 49¼ in.) Madrid, Prado (No.1166).
The Madonna is painted from the same model as in
No.4. – The picture is not signed but the date 1619 is inscribed below the feet of the Madonna.

9. THE FRANCISCAN NUN, DOÑA JERÓ-
NIMA DE LA FUENTE. 1620. (160× 110 cm.; 63
× 43¼ in.) Madrid, Prado (No.2873).
From the Convent of Santa Isabel de los Reyes, Toledo;
since 1944 in the Prado. Dated 1620. A variant of this
portrait is in the collection of Alejandro Fernández de
Araoz, Madrid.

10-11. THE DRINKERS ('Los Borrachos'). About
1628. (165× 225 cm.; 65× 88⅝ in.) Madrid, Prado
(No. 1170).
The picture is also called 'The Triumph of Bacchus'.
First mentioned in the Inventory of the Alcázar of 1636.
The composition has some indefinable relationship with
paintings of the same subject by Rubens (who, in 1628,
visited Madrid), while the figure of Bacchus recalls the
Bacchus by Caravaggio in the Villa Borghese in Rome.
None the less, the picture is highly original, and there is
nothing even in Velazquez's own work with which to
compare it. It was painted before his first journey to Italy,
and then retouched after his return, in 1631 or not much
later.

12. THE FORGE OF VULCAN. 1630. (223×290 cm.; 87¾×114 in.) Madrid, Prado (No.1171). Painted in Rome in 1630, probably retouched a few years later. Bought for King Philip IV in 1634.

The painting 'Jacob receiving the blood-stained coat of Joseph' (Escorial) is usually regarded as the companion piece to the 'Forge of Vulcan'.

The picture represents Apollo informing Vulcan of the adultery of his wife Venus with Mars. On the right four Cyclopes as assistants in Vulcan's forge.

13-14. CHRIST AFTER THE FLAGELLA-TION. About 1631. (165×206 cm.; 65×81¼ in.) London, National Gallery (No.1148).

In the centre, Christ (according to Neil Maclaren rather reminiscent of Guido Reni); on the right the Christian Soul, in the form of an innocent child contemplating the suffering Christ; behind the child its guardian angel.

Probably painted during the artist's first visit to Italy and retouched soon after his return to Madrid. Bought 1858 in Madrid by an English collector and later presented to the National Gallery.

15. CHRIST ON THE CROSS. Detail. (The figure in the painting is life-size.) About 1631-32. Madrid, Prado (No.1167).

From the Convent of San Plácido in Madrid; since 1829 in the Prado.

The wide background of the picture, a landscape, has turned almost black. The figure, or at least the part repro-duced here, is in a very good state of preservation.

Another, much smaller, version of *Christ on the Cross* (Prado No.2903) appears to be signed and dated 1631.

16-17. THE TEMPTATION OF SAINT THOMAS AQUINAS. About 1631-32. (244×203 cm.; 96×80 in.) Orihuela, Cathedral Museum.

The picture was discovered in 1906 by Elías Tormo in the College of Orihuela and attributed to Nicolás de Villacis; later Tormo declared it to be a joint work of Alonso Cano and Velazquez; to judge from the style of the painting, this is convincing (see Introduction,p.13). Allende-Salazar and Lafuente Ferrari regard it as painted completely by Velazquez's own hand.

The College of Preachers of the Order of St. Dominic, the Orihuela University, received in 1632 a number of paintings they had ordered some time before. As it is generally assumed that *The Temptation of St. Thomas Aquinas* was one of those paintings, it must be dated accordingly.

The following episode from the life of the Saint is repre-sented in this picture. His brothers, the Counts of

Aquino, tried by every means to prevent him from entering the order of St. Dominic; they imprisoned him for two years in their castle, the Rocca-Secca in the Kingdom of Naples, and one day they sent a courtesan to seduce him. But his prayers overcame temptation and angels rescued him by girding his loins with a sash.

18. PRINCE BALTASAR CARLOS WITH HIS DWARF. About 1631. (136×104 cm.; 53½×41 in.) Boston, Museum of Fine Arts (No. 01.104).

The Prince, son of King Philip IV and his first wife Queen Isabella de Bourbon, was born 17 October 1629. This portrait shows him at an age of about two. The dwarf's name was Francisco Lezcano, called 'the Biscayan'.

19. PRINCE BALTASAR CARLOS. About 1632 (118×95 cm.; 46¼×37½ in.) London, Wallace Collection (No.12).

Reproduced here in the present state, without the tassel and other later additions, which were removed when the picture was cleaned before the last war.

20. KING PHILIP IV IN BROWN AND SILVER. About 1632-34. (Size increased by later addi-tions; 200×113 cm.; 78½×44½ in.) London, National Gallery (No.1129).

The picture is fully signed. In 1936 it was cleaned and a dark varnish removed.

21. THE COURT JESTER DON JUAN DE AUSTRIA. About 1634. (210×123 cm.; 82½×48½ in.) Madrid, Prado (No.1200).

The earliest picture in the series of Court Jesters which Velazquez painted between 1634 and 1644. This buffoon was called in mockery after the victor of Lepanto; appar-ently he was fond of armour and dressed like a warrior. The room opens on to a view of the sea and a naval battle.

22. THE CARDINAL-INFANTE DON FER-NANDO AS A HUNTER. About 1632-35. (191× 107 cm.; 75¼×42⅛ in.) Madrid, Prado (No.1186).

The Cardinal-Infante, a brother of the King, was born in 1609. In 1632 he left Madrid and went to Brussels as Governor of the Low Countries, where he died in 1641. He never visited Madrid during the last nine years of his life. As this portrait – like the other two belonging to the same series – was finished at the earliest in 1635, it must either have been begun before the Cardinal-Infante left Madrid, or else the head was painted after another portrait of him.

The three 'Portraits in Hunting Dress' (of the King, his son, and his brother) were intended as a decoration for he Torre de la Parada, a Royal hunting lodge.

3. PRINCE BALTASAR CARLOS AS A HUNTER. 1635–36. (Detail, omitting parts of the background. The figure in the painting is life-size.) Madrid, Prado (No.1189).

The picture is inscribed 'anno aetatis suae VI', and as the Prince was born on the 17 October 1629, this portrait can be dated 1635–36. A smaller version of this portrait at Ickworth, Suffolk (Marquis of Bristol, now National Trust; KdK 177) shows three dogs at the right.

4–26. THE SURRENDER OF BREDA ('Las Lanzas'). 1634–35. (307×367 cm.; 121×144½ in.) Madrid, Prado (No. 1172).

See the Introduction, p. 9.

In June 1625 Count Justin of Nassau surrendered Breda to the Spaniards. (Breda, a stronghold of the Dutch, had been besieged for ten months.) Only two years after Velazquez had finished his great painting Breda was free again. The picture was intended for the 'Hall of the Kingdoms' in the Buen Retiro Palace, which was inaugurated in 1635, at which time 'Las Lanzas' must have been finished. When Velazquez painted this picture both generals were no longer alive; Spinola had died in the autumn 1630, Justin of Nassau in the following year. The two central figures in 'Las Lanzas', looking so true to life, were probably painted from some indifferent portraits.

7–28. SAINT ANTHONY ABBOT AND SAINT PAUL THE HERMIT. About 1641–43. 257×188 cm.; 101×74 in.) Madrid, Prado (No.1169).

Painted for the Hermitage of St. Paul in the gardens of the Buen Retiro Palace. The dating of this painting is still disputed, and Velazquez may have retouched it after his return from his second Italian journey; technically it shows similarities with works by some contemporary Italian painters, such as Andrea Sacchi.

The picture combines several scenes. (A so-called 'continuous representation', depicting a number of successive incidents in the background and in the foreground of the same picture.) At the left, in the far background: St. Anthony meeting the centaur and the satyr. In the centre background: St. Anthony arriving at the cave and knocking at the door which is let into the rock. The main scene in the foreground: The two hermit saints; St. Paul relates how a raven – who is just passing the top of the rock – has brought him half a loaf of bread every day during sixty years. In the left lower corner: two lions digging a grave for St. Paul.

As Lafuente Ferrari has observed, the picture was originally in a frame with semicircular top (of which some faint marks are impressed in the upper corners).

29. THE CORONATION OF THE VIRGIN. About 1641–43. (176×124 cm.; 69½×49 in.) Madrid, Prado (No.1168).

Painted for the Queen's oratory in the Alcázar, an anteroom of the New Palace at Madrid. A date ante quem is given for the picture by the free repetition painted by Jusepe Martinez, a pupil of Velazquez, in 1644 for the Saragossa Cathedral (Allende-Salazar, KdK, 1925, p. 279, note to p. 104).

On the left, Christ, holding a sceptre; on the right, God the Father, holding the globe of universe; over the Virgin's head, the Holy Spirit, witnessing the coronation.

30. MARS. About 1642–44. (179×95 cm.; 70½×37½ in.) Madrid, Prado (No.1208).

Painted for the Torre de la Parada, a Royal hunting lodge, for which Rubens also delivered a number of pictures in 1638 (Oldenburg, Rubens, KdK, 4th edition, pp. 392–393). Velazquez's Mars looks almost like a pendant to Rubens's Vulcan (Prado, No. 1676). Both pictures are of the same dimensions, and both are inspired by the same anti-classical feeling.

31. THE COURT JESTER DON DIEGO DE ACEDO, CALLED EL PRIMO. 1644. (107×82 cm.; 41⅛×32¼ in.) Madrid, Prado (No.1201).

Painted at the same time as the 'Fraga Portrait' (Plate 33).

32. PRINCE BALTASAR CARLOS. About 1640–42. (128.5×99 cm.; 50½×39 in.) Vienna, Kunsthistorisches Museum (Cat. No.733, Inv. No.312).

See note on plate 18. – A. L. Mayer, E. du Gué Trapier, and other writers assume that parts of the painting are by the hand of an assistant.

33. KING PHILIP IV AT FRAGA. 1644. (133.5× 98.5 cm.; 52½×40 in.) New York, Frick Collection (No.123).

Painted at Fraga in Aragon, when Velazquez accompanied the King during the campaign of 1644. Palomino (1724) saw the picture still in the Royal Palace at Madrid; later it belonged to the Duke of Parma; Henry Clay Frick bought it from a Private Collection in Vienna.

The lower end of the picture is cut by at least 4 inches. A very good contemporary copy is at Dulwich College.

34. THE SCULPTOR JUAN MARTÍNEZ MONTAÑÉS. About 1648. (109×107 cm.; 42⅞×42⅛ in.) Madrid, Prado (No.1194).

According to Lafuente Ferrari the picture was originally much larger and was cut down on all four sides.

Montañés was called from Sevilla to the Court of Madrid in 1636 to make a model of the head of the King for his equestrian bronze monument, which was commissioned from Pietro Tacca in Florence. Allende-Salazar dated the picture from this period, but Beruete dated it 'some ten or twelve years later', and A. L. Mayer remarked: 'The difficulty is that the brushwork is not at all in the style of Velazquez of the period (1636–37), and corresponds much more closely with the late style of the master.' Perhaps it was sketched in during Montañés's stay at Madrid in 1636 and continued much later. The picture is still not quite finished. Montañés died in 1649.

35. THE LADY WITH A FAN. About 1648. (93× 68 cm.; 36½×26⅞ in.) London, Wallace Collection (No.88).

According to Aureliano de Beruete (1898), this is a portrait of Velazquez's daughter Francisca, who married the painter Juan Bautista Martínez del Mazo. The same model is represented in a fine portrait which was probably painted by Mazo with some help from his father-in-law (Chatsworth, Duke of Devonshire; *Velazquez*, KdK 201; Exhibition Madrid 1960, No.129).

36. MERCURY AND ARGUS. About 1659. (127 × 248 cm.; 50×98 in.) Madrid, Prado (No.1175).

The dating of this picture is based on Palomino (1724), who has recorded that in 1659 the 'Hall of the Mirrors' in the Royal Palace, the Alcázar, was decorated with mythological paintings by various artists; Velazquez was in charge of this undertaking and contributed four pictures of his own. All the paintings were lost in a fire of 1734, only a fragment of 'Mercury and Argus' was saved; the upper 14 inches are not original but have been added after the fire. The companion piece was a 'Apollo flaying Marsyas'; the other two pictures by Velazquez represented 'Cupid and Psyche', and 'Venus and Adonis'.

37. THE TOILET OF VENUS ('The Rokeby Venus'). About 1650. (123×177 cm.; 48×70 in.) London, National Gallery (No.2057).

Painted probably during the artist's second visit to Italy; inspired by similar Titian pictures. Recorded already in 1651 in the collection of a Spanish nobleman. The subject is connected with 'Venus and Adonis' (see note on plate 36), which, however, was of a later date, and is lost as are all the other paintings of female nudes by Velazquez.

The figure of Venus was cut in seven places by a suffragette demonstrator in 1914; the repairs are faintly visible. There is an older tear across the small of the back of Venus, and this part is also restored.

38. VIEW FROM THE VILLA MEDICI IN ROME, MIDDAY. 1650. (44×38 cm.; 17⅜×15 in.) Madrid, Prado (No.1211).

This landscape and the companion piece (plate 39) were painted during Velazquez's second stay in Italy.

39. VIEW FROM THE VILLA MEDICI IN ROME, EVENING. 1650. (48×42 cm.; 19×16½in.) Madrid, Prado (No.1210).

See the note on plate 38.

40. POPE INNOCENT X. 1650. (140×120 cm.; 55¼×47¼ in.) Rome, Galleria Doria Pamphili.

On June 23, 1786, Reynolds wrote to the Duke of Rutland about a painting which the Duke had acquired, a version, or rather a copy, of this portrait: 'At Chiswick there is likewise a head of the same Pope by Velasques, but not equal to that which is at Rome, which I think is one of the first portraits in the world.' (Reynolds is always misquoted as having said 'the most beautiful picture in Rome'.) Another version is in the collection of the Duke of Devonshire; and the best copies of the head are in the National Gallery of Art in Washington, in the Wellington Museum in London, and another one (by Juan de Pareja) in the Isabella Stewart Gardner Museum, Boston. All those copies have, at one time or the other, been regarded as authentic paintings.

The portrait in the Galleria Doria Pamphili is fully signed on the letter the Pope is holding: '... Per Diego de Silva Velazquez de la Camera di S. Mta. Cattca'.

41. THE INFANTA MARGARITA. About 1653. (128.5×100 cm.; 50½×39½ in.) Vienna, Kunsthistorisches Museum (Cat. No.736, Inv. No.321).

Daughter of King Philip IV and his second wife, Maria Anna of Austria; born 1651.

A variant of this portrait, without the vase of flowers (cf. plate II), is in the collection of the Duke of Alba, Madrid (Velazquez Exhibition 1960, No.77; illustrated).

42. THE MAIDS OF HONOUR ('Las Meninas'). 1656. (318×276 cm.; 125×118½ in.) Madrid, Prado (No.1174).

See the Introduction, p. 15. The Santiago Cross on the breast of Velazquez (cf. plate I) is a later addition. (Velazquez was made a Knight of the Order of Santiago three years after he finished this painting.)

According to A. L. Mayer the picture was damaged in the fire of 1734 and restored by Juan de Miranda, especially in the upper right corner.

In the background, over the royal couple in the mirror, two paintings by Rubens.

43. A MAID OF HONOUR (Doña Isabel de Velasco). Detail from plate 42.

44. THE TAPESTRY WEAVERS ('Las Hiland-eras'). About 1657–59. (220×289 cm.; 86½×113½ in.) Madrid, Prado (No.1173).
See Introduction p. 15f.
The picture has suffered in the fire of 1734; later additions at the top and on the left.

45. THE TAPESTRY WEAVERS. Detail from plate 44.

46. THE INFANTA MARGARITA IN BLUE. 1659. (127×107 cm.; 50×42⅛ in.) Wien, Kunsthistorisches Museum (Cat. No.739, Inv. No.2130).
See the note on plate 41. The Princess is portrayed here at the age of eight. Painted together with the portrait of her brother (plate 48) and sent as a present from the Court

of Madrid to the Court of Vienna. In the 18th century the picture had been cut down to fit into an oval frame. In 1924 the picture was restored and the missing corners added.

47. THE INFANTA MARGARITA. Detail from plate 46.

48. PRINCE PHILIP PROSPER. 1659. (128.5× 99.5 cm.; 50½×39 in.) Vienna, Kunsthistorisches Museum (Cat. No.738, Inv. No.319).
Companion piece to plate 46.
The Infante, the third child of King Philip and Maria Anna of Austria, was born on the 28 December 1657; he died when he was not yet four years old.
A detail: Plate III.

THE THREE COLOUR PLATES *in the text part of this book are details from plates 41, 42 and 48 respectively.*

LIST OF COLLECTIONS